Breakthroughs in Science

by Jenny Green

Contents

Longman

Edinburgh Gate
Harlow, Essex

Foreword

Have you ever looked at the world around you and wondered how it got to be that way, how it works, and what would happen if …?

Scientists are like you.

Most scientific breakthroughs are the work of more than one person. Scientists always learn from the work of other scientists, sometimes by proving them wrong.

This is what Newton meant when he said, "If I have seen further it is because I have stood on the shoulders of giants."

The Survival of the Fittest

Have you ever watched different birds fly past? Have you sat in a garden and looked at the different types of plants, animals and insects? We know of at least two million different kinds of living things. In the eighteenth century, a Swedish botanist called Carolus Linnaeus created a two-part system to describe and name living things. The names are all in Latin and each name has two parts. The first part shows the **type** of plant or animal, and the second part shows the **species**. We still use this system today.

Common Daisy
Bellis perennis

Common House-fly
Musca domestica

Robin
Erithacus rubecula

What is a Species?

A species is a group of living things that are alike enough to produce offspring which can reproduce themselves. For example, all human beings belong to one species called *homo sapiens*. People who look very different can have children together. Those children can have their own children when they grow up.

Learning About Species and Evolution

Three hundred years ago, many people thought God had made the Earth in seven days. They thought God had made all species and that species did not change. They believed that fossils such as dinosaur skeletons were either the remains of earlier creations or of creatures still alive somewhere. A bishop had worked out from the dates in the Bible that God created the Earth in 4004 BC. But in 1830, Charles Lyell in his book *Principles of Geology* said that the Earth was much older. He pointed out that the sea wears away cliffs, and earthquakes change the shape of the land. He said that natural processes like rainfall shaped the land over a very long time.

In 1831, Charles Darwin (1809–1882) took Lyell's book to read on a long sea voyage. Darwin had studied to become a clergyman, but he enjoyed nature and geology more. Now he was going to be a naturalist on a Royal Navy round-the-world expedition. He had to make notes and drawings and collect samples of animals, plants, fossils and rocks.

HMS Beagle sailed for South America in December 1831, and Darwin was so seasick that he could only lie down and read. What he read in Lyell's book impressed him very much.

Darwin was amazed by the huge variety of wildlife in the Brazilian rainforest. In Argentina and Patagonia he found fossils of extinct creatures like the Megatherium (giant sloth). Why had it died out? What was the connection between it and living creatures, he wondered?

As HMS Beagle sailed around the southern tip of South America, Darwin noticed how the plants, animals and people adapted to changes in the climate. At a port in Chile, he saw an earthquake lift the land around the harbour a metre higher above the sea. So when Darwin later found fossils of sea creatures in the Andes mountains, he realised they must have taken thousands of years to lift that high.

When the Beagle arrived at the Galapagos Islands, Darwin found strange species of wildlife such as giant tortoises. They were like tortoises on the mainland but none of them was exactly the same and each island had its own species. Darwin was particularly interested by some small brown birds called finches. Finches on different islands had differently-shaped beaks to help them tackle the food that was most common on that island. Some had big beaks to crack tough seeds, while others had long slim beaks for catching insects.

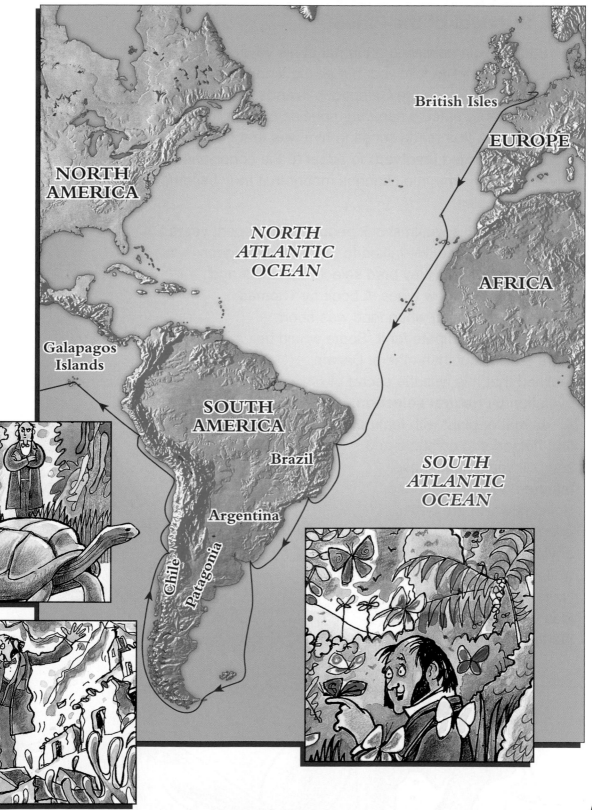

NORTH
AMERICA

British Isles

EUROPE

NORTH
ATLANTIC
OCEAN

AFRICA

Galapagos
Islands

SOUTH
AMERICA

Brazil

SOUTH
ATLANTIC
OCEAN

Argentina

Chile

Patagonia

The Survival of the Fittest

In 1836, Darwin published a journal of his voyage. Books about geology and wildlife followed, but all the time he thought about what he had seen on the Galapagos Islands. He could not believe that God had created a separate species of finch for each island. The only idea that made sense to him was that the finches had gradually changed (**evolved**) to adapt to the conditions they lived in. After a long time, the changes meant that they became different species.

Darwin knew this would shock people, so he spent years gathering evidence. He talked to farmers and pigeon keepers about how they bred selected animals and birds to produce new types. A book by Thomas Malthus argued that when food was short, people would compete for it. Some would be more successful than others. Darwin realised that this was the secret of evolution by **natural selection**. An animal or plant with features that helped it to compete and survive would pass those features on to its offspring. Species which are better adapted to the environment survive, while others die out. He later called this idea 'the survival of the fittest'.

In 1859, Darwin published his book *On the Origin of Species by Means of Natural Selection*. It described how species evolved by passing on to their offspring the features that helped them to survive. Species that could not adapt to their environment and compete for food died out.

Darwin's theory upset many people because they thought it contradicted the Bible. They realised that his theory meant humans evolved from the same ancestors as apes. Some people felt insulted because they thought Darwin meant humans had descended from apes. Gradually, though, most scientists accepted the theory. When Darwin published *The Descent of Man* in 1871, there was much less fuss.

How Do Species Change by Evolution?

Darwin showed that species changed by evolution, but he could not explain exactly how this happened. The answer lay in the work of an Austrian monk called Gregor Mendel. He kept careful records of his experiments in breeding pea plants of different heights and colours. He showed that some features were more likely to appear in the offspring than others, and that this followed predictable rules. Although Mendel worked at the same time as Darwin, his work was not recognised until 1900. It was the beginning of the new science of **genetics**.

Scientists still believe that life evolved through adaptation and natural selection, but now they think the process was not always gradual. Sometimes species stay the same for a long time and then change quickly if the environment changes. However, the story of evolution has not finished. There is more to discover, and the life we see around us is still evolving.

Learning How to Learn

Galileo, Newton and the Scientific Method

If somebody tells you something, or you read it in a book, how do you know if it is true?

Philosophers like Aristotle in ancient Greece believed that they could answer any question by reasoning and argument. But they had no way to test their theories. The greatest scientific breakthroughs happened after people learned the scientific method of experiment and observation.

Until the sixteenth century, people believed that the Sun, Moon, stars and planets circled the Earth. Astronomers noticed that Mars, Jupiter and Saturn sometimes seemed to move backwards but they did not know why. Then a Polish astronomer, Nicolaus Copernicus (1473–1543), said that if the Earth and other planets circled the Sun, spinning as they went, this explained what they saw. Few people believed him, because his ideas went against the Bible and the beliefs of ancient Greek philosophers.

Testing Theories

An Italian mathematician, Galileo Galilei (1564–1642), began to think that the ancient Greeks had sometimes been wrong. Aristotle had written that heavy objects fall much faster than light ones. However, when Galileo climbed the Leaning Tower of Pisa and dropped two objects of different weights at the same time, they landed almost together.

Galileo made careful measurements. He found he could use mathematics to predict how things fell and also the movements of pendulums and tides. This was a new way of testing theories, but Galileo's theories only worked if Copernicus had been right about the planets circling the Sun.

In 1609, Galileo heard about a new invention: the telescope. He built one that magnified things twenty times and saw mountains and craters on the Moon. He also saw four of Jupiter's moons and the stars of the Milky Way. Watching changes in the planet Venus convinced him that Copernicus had been correct.

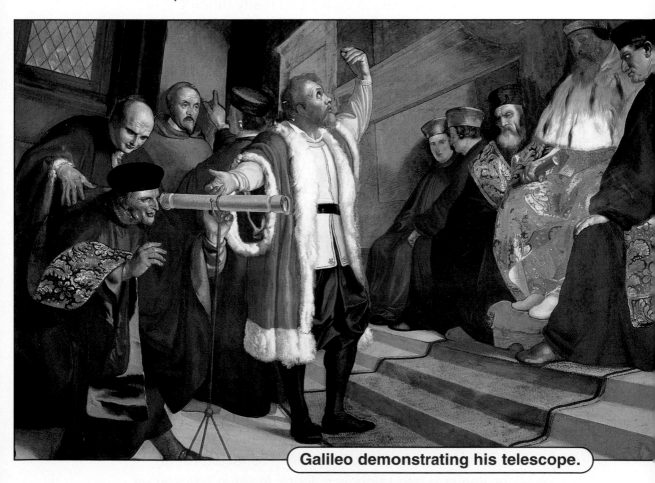

Galileo demonstrating his telescope.

In 1632, Galileo published a book which discussed whether the Earth or the Sun was the centre of the universe. The idea that the Earth moves around the Sun contradicted the teaching of the Church. Galileo was arrested, forced to say he was mistaken, and his book was burned. Galileo went back to studying motion and mechanics.

Finding Proof

The German astronomer Johannes Kepler (1571–1630) had also accepted Copernicus' ideas. By observing Mars he worked out how planets moved:

- Planets orbit the Sun in elliptical (oval) paths.

- The closer a planet comes to the Sun, the faster it moves.

- All planets have the same relationship between their distance from the Sun and the time they take to complete one orbit.

Kepler's writings and calculations convinced many other astronomers that Copernicus had been right.

Scientists like Galileo and Kepler began a new way of finding out about the world. They made observations and experiments, they tested ideas and analysed results and used them to devise new theories. By the time that Isaac Newton was born in 1642, many scholars accepted their work and the new scientific method.

The Discoveries of Isaac Newton

At Cambridge University, Newton soon overtook his teachers in mathematics. He read books by Copernicus, Galileo and Kepler, and a book by the philosopher Descartes which said we should only accept something if it seemed proved beyond doubt. When the university closed because of plague in 1665 and 1666, Newton studied at home.

In 1665, Newton used the experimental method to test his theory about light. Aristotle had said that white light was a single pure substance, and people believed that prisms or raindrops added the colours of the spectrum. Newton, however, thought white light was a mixture of different coloured rays. He shone a narrow ray of sunlight through a prism. As it left the prism it refracted (bent), became wider and split into rainbow colours. Newton blocked all but one of the colours and shone that through another prism. It did not change, and so showed that all the light rays of one colour could not split any further.

Newton conducting his prism experiment.

At the same time, Newton worked on a mathematical technique which is now called **calculus**. It deals with numbers that change, and describes how objects move. Using this, he worked out his Laws of Motion, published in the 1670s.

- An object stays still, or carries on moving as it is, unless some force acts on it. If you throw a ball in space, it continues in a straight line. But if you throw a ball into the air on Earth, air resistance slows it, and the force of gravity pulls it down.

- If a force acts on an object, the object moves in the direction of that force. It accelerates according to the strength of the force and the mass* of the object. A ball moves in the direction you kick it. If you kick it harder, it accelerates faster. A big, heavy ball goes slower than a small, light ball.

- For every action there is an equal and opposite reaction. If two balls crash into each other, they rebound according to how fast they collide.

Newton thought that there was an invisible attraction between objects. Some people say the idea came when he watched an apple fall from a tree and wondered why apples never fell upwards. He thought that objects with a bigger mass would have a stronger force of attraction. The Earth is very large so it has a very strong force pulling things towards its centre. We call this force **gravity**. Newton's law of gravitation says that all objects have an attracting force.

* Mass is a measurement of how much force is needed to change an object's speed or direction. A larger mass needs a larger force.

Newton's laws account for the way the Moon orbits the Earth. The Moon would go in a straight line unless some force acted on it. Earth's gravity pulls it towards the Earth.

In 1687 Newton's greatest book, the *Principia*, gave scientists a simple set of laws and rules to describe events that seemed unconnected. It built on Galileo and Kepler's work, and explained processes from the orbits of planets to the movement of tides and things falling to the Earth.

Like Galileo, Newton realised that mathematics was the basic language of science, and used it to describe his discoveries. The poet Alexander Pope wrote about him:

Nature and Nature's laws lay hid in night:
God said, "Let Newton be!" and all was light.

People used Newton's laws and equations for over two hundred years. Eventually scientists found areas that did not fit the facts exactly, but they still explain much of what happens in the world around us.

Space, Time, Light and Power

Time and Motion

How do you know if you are moving? When you drive in a car you sit still. If you look out of the car window you can see that you are moving but the road is standing still. You are moving relative to the road. Because the Earth moves around the Sun, you move at around 107,000 km per hour relative to the Sun even when you are asleep in bed!

When Isaac Newton wrote his laws of motion in the 1670s he had to describe how motion worked with space and time. Newton thought that time was always the same and always flowed in the same direction. He said we measure time by motion, and motion relative to a point in space. We measure days by the movement of the Earth around the Sun. When you travel from home to school, you travel through time as well as space. You set out at one time, and arrive later.

The Theories of Relativity

Later scientists tried to understand how energy worked together with mass* and motion. They believed that time was always the same everywhere in the universe. But gradually, astronomers found areas where Newton's laws did not fit. Albert Einstein (1879–1955) developed theories of relativity which changed the way people thought about the universe and time.

When you look at the night sky, you look back in time. The light you see has taken many years to reach you from even the nearest stars. Astronomers looking at the distant Andromeda galaxy see it as it was when the light left it two million years ago. Einstein wondered how the universe would look to somebody sitting on a beam of light, travelling as fast as the light did. Light travels faster than anything else in the universe: 300,000 km per second.

* Mass is a measurement of how much force is needed to change an object's speed or direction. A larger mass needs a larger force.

14

Anything travelling faster than light would go back in time. Einstein based his theories on experiments done in his head or using mathematics. Later on, real experiments proved him correct.

Einstein's famous formula $E=mc^2$ means that mass and energy can turn into each other. Light is a form of energy, so if we travelled away from Earth at nearly the speed of light, strange things would happen. Our mass would increase enormously, and we would not be able to keep accelerating. Time would slow down for the travellers, but for the people on Earth it would carry on normally. When we came back, we would find that everyone else was a lot older.

If we could travel at the speed of light, time would stop for us altogether. If we could travel faster than light, we would go back in time.

Nuclear energy

Einstein's work also revealed a new source of power. Energy binds together the parts of an atom, including the central part called the **nucleus**. The nucleus of an atom is tiny, but Einstein's work showed that very little mass could release a huge amount of energy. When one nucleus splits apart, it splits other nuclei around it. This is called a **chain reaction**. A team of scientists led by Enrico Fermi showed that they could control the energy which was released when they split apart a nucleus of a particular type of uranium.

In 1939, Einstein suggested to the American President that nuclear reactions could generate electricity or make a bomb. He thought nobody would ever use such a bomb, but that the threat of one would stop an enemy. During World War II the Americans fought the Japanese. A team of scientists led by J. Robert Oppenheimer developed atomic bombs, but the Japanese would not surrender. They refused to believe that the bomb was so powerful. Einstein was horrified when the Americans used a nuclear bomb to destroy the Japanese city of Hiroshima. Eighty thousand people died. Scientists only realised how deadly nuclear radiation was when 60,000 more people died within a year from radiation sickness.

After the war, scientists could see that the world would run out of coal, gas and oil one day. They hoped nuclear energy would provide cheap electric power, but nuclear power stations created problems for society. If there was an accident, radiation could poison the land for many miles around. It is also difficult to store radioactive waste safely.

Fusion power

Now scientists are investigating other kinds of atomic power. **Nuclear fusion** releases energy when nuclei collide and combine. This kind of reaction powers the Sun and other stars. Fusion reactions use hydrogen, which is plentiful and cheap, and they do not produce radioactive waste. So far, scientists have not been able to build a fusion reactor that will produce energy cheaply and easily, but if they can solve the problems fusion reactors could be the power source of the future.

The World in Your Living Room: Computers and the Internet

How is Your Brain like a Computer?

Your brain gets information through your senses. A computer gets information through things that plug into it, such as a keyboard and cables. Computers store information on disks or silicon chips just as your brain stores information in its pathways. Your brain can work out things it doesn't already know. A computer can only use information you put into it, but it can do that much faster than most people.

The Development of Computers

Long ago, people used tools such as an abacus or a slide rule to help them calculate faster. However, they could only store instructions or data by writing them down.

In 1801, a French weaver called Joseph Jacquard developed a loom that used large cards with holes punched into them to program the pattern. Later, Charles Babbage used the idea of storing instructions on punched cards in his **Difference Engine**. This machine could deal with complicated sums. Modern computers use some of his ideas, though Babbage never actually made a working model.

Augusta Ada Lovelace, daughter of the poet Lord Byron, translated an Italian paper about Babbage's designs. She added notes to explain them and did calculations for Babbage. A modern computer language is called ADA in her honour.

In 1890, the US census office held a competition to find a better way to deal with information. The census office counts people and collects data about them. They took seven years to process the 1880 census information by hand. Now that there were more people, the census office worried that publishing the information would take too long. Herman Hollerith invented a mechanical calculator that used punched cards like Babbage's machine. Using

18

this method they published the census results in six weeks. These machines became even faster once electronic valves were invented. They could do a multiplication in one second, but they could only do simple calculations.

Then in 1936, a British mathematician called Alan Turing wrote about how to use logical rules in calculating machines. His team built the world's first computer at Bletchley Park during World War II to break the secret German codes. They named it **Colossus**. It contained 6000 electronic valves and used Turing's rules to sort through data stored on punched tape.

Colossus

By 1946, the American computer ENIAC could do 100,000 calculations a second. However, it weighed 30 tonnes and contained 18,000 electronic valves which often burned out. Transistors, developed by William Shockley and his colleagues in 1947, were much smaller and more reliable. The modern version is the silicon chip using millions of transistors in a tiny space.

Operators had to rewire early computers to use different programs. Modern computing began when scientists at Manchester University in 1948 designed a computer that would store programs and data, although floppy disks did not appear until 1971.

Computer Language

Just as you only understand people who use your language, a computer can only understand instructions in its own language. At first, people had to use **machine code** to program computers. It was hard to learn. In 1951 Grace Murray Hopper of the US Navy developed a computer language that people could understand, which computers could translate into machine code. She began the phrase "a bug in the program" for a fault, when an early program of hers crashed after a moth got caught in the computer.

In the 1970s, Bill Gates invented a language called BASIC that was even easier and meant more people could use computers at home. He also developed an operating system called MS-DOS. Operating systems are sets of instructions that tell a computer how to work. Because these were very popular, Gates' company, Microsoft, became the largest computer company in the world.

On the early computers, people programmed simple games that would seem boring today. One game called Pong was just two bats hitting a ball backwards and forwards. Adventure games were just text on a screen, like an electronic adventure game book. To make pictures move realistically on a screen takes a lot of memory. Home computers have only had this much power recently.

Computer chips can now control household appliances and cars. Modern home computers are over two thousand times more powerful than the computer in the Apollo spacecraft that landed on the moon in 1969. Now that computers are smaller and cheaper, more households own them. People can use them for work and games and to explore the Internet.

The Internet

In 1969, telephone lines linked American universities in a network so their computers could communicate with each other. Within four years, universities outside America joined in. The international network (Internet) grew as more computers could link through central computers called **servers**.

When you connect to the Internet, you use the World Wide Web. On a page of information (a web page) you can often see links to other pages. These are like doors into another room, but the room could be anywhere in the world on any sort of computer. This is possible because in 1989 physicist Tim Berners-Lee wanted a way for scientists to share information. He invented a language called **http** that allowed one computer to read data stored on any other computer. When an Internet address begins http, the computer knows this is the language to use.

Many people connect home computers to the Internet. They can create their own web pages about things that interest them, and find other people with simliar interests. They can use electronic mail (e-mail) to write to anybody else linked to the Internet. Companies sell goods and services over the net. Newspapers call this the **information superhighway**.

The Internet is exciting. It is like having the whole world in your own home, with libraries, shops, cinemas and friends to chat with. You have to learn how to find information, as you would in any library. Anybody can put web pages on the Internet, so the information you find is not always accurate. You have to use common sense to judge it. Because people all over the world can share their interests regardless of race, sex, age or religion, it is the first truly international community.

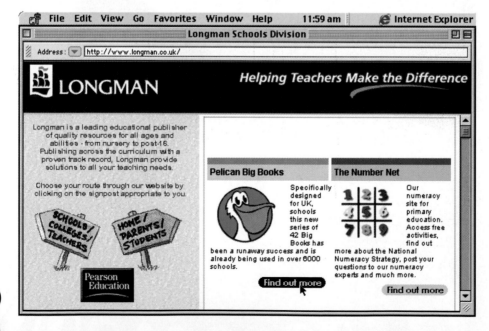

The Double Helix

Characteristics Are Passed On

Why do you look like your parents but different from your friends?

The answer begins with Gregor Mendel. He was an Austrian monk who studied pea plants. By transferring pollen (pollinating) he crossed tall plants with short plants. The first generation of offspring were all tall. Mendel called this the **dominant** form. He called the short form **recessive**, because it seemed to disappear.

Mendel pollinated the first generation of pea plants with itself. In the second generation, short plants reappeared. He found there were always three tall plants to every short plant. Mendel proved that parents passed on characteristics to offspring predictably, but how?

Cells are the building blocks of life. All living things start as single fertilised cells that keep dividing. Scientists identified tiny threads, which they called **chromosomes** (from the Greek words for coloured bodies) in the central part or nucleus of cells. All human cells contain 23 matching pairs. American biologists suggested that chromosomes were linked groups of factors called **genes** that held the secret of inheritance.

The Discovery of DNA

In the late 19th century Friedrich Miescher discovered several proteins and an unusual acid in the nucleus of cells. The scientific name of the acid is deoxyribonucleic acid, or DNA. In 1944 American biologists Alfred Hershey and Martha Chase experimented with bacteria to show that DNA passed genes from one generation to the next.

How could this molecule hold all the information controlling the development of humans, animals and plants? It contained four chemical bases called adenine (A), thymine (T), guanine (G) and cytosine (C), plus phosphoric acid and a sugar. Erwin Chargaff proved there were always equal amounts of A and T and of G and C in cells, but nobody knew how they fitted together.

British scientists Rosalind Franklin and Maurice Wilkins passed X-rays through DNA. By studying the patterns made when the crystals bent (diffracted) the X-rays, Rosalind Franklin concluded that DNA must be a spiral shape (helix). James Watson and Francis Crick, working in Cambridge, used this information to help them solve the puzzle of DNA structure. They built a model showing that if A always paired with T, and G paired with C, DNA must be like a ladder made of two strands twisted together in a double helix. The sugar and phosphoric acid were the sides of the ladder, and the rungs were the paired bases.

Watson and Crick suggested that DNA could separate into two strands and that each acted as a pattern to grow a new strand. Groups of three bases called codons on each strand make the codes for different amino acids. Amino acids are chemicals that make the thousands of different proteins that build the different types of cell in your body.

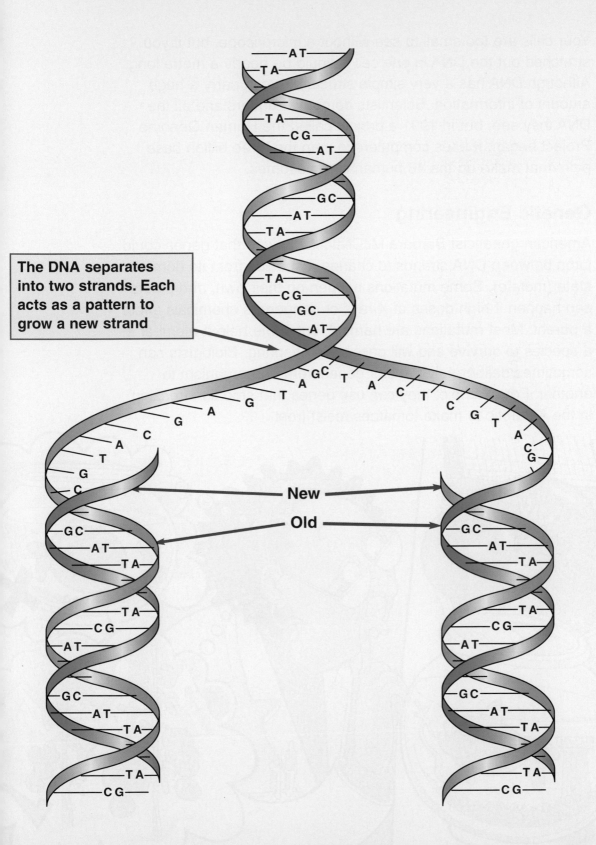

The DNA separates into two strands. Each acts as a pattern to grow a new strand

New

Old

Your cells are too small to see without a microscope, but if you stretched out the DNA in one cell it would be nearly a metre long. Although DNA has a very simple structure, it can carry a huge amount of information. Scientists do not yet understand all the DNA they see, but in 1991 a project called the Human Genome Project began. It uses computers to map the three billion base pairs that make up the 46 human chromosomes.

Genetic Engineering

American geneticist Barbara McClintock showed that genes could jump between DNA strands to change a species from its normal state (mutate). Some mutations happen on their own, and others can happen if high doses of X-rays or dangerous chemicals affect a parent. Most mutations are harmful, but some help a member of a species to survive and will pass to its offspring. Biologists can sometimes deliberately transfer genes from one organism to another. For example, they can use genes that stop fish freezing in the Antarctic to make tomatoes resist frost.

Is **genetic engineering** a good idea? Some people believe that modifying crops to improve the vitamin content or make them resist drought or weedkillers will help us grow more and better food. Others believe we know too little about what might happen if we alter nature in ways it could not alter itself. They think it is too risky to grow such plants where they might cross-breed with others. Many people worry that designing people genetically might change the human race in ways we cannot foresee. Most countries still have laws to prevent scientists researching genetic engineering in humans.

Using DNA

Understanding genes can help people. Genetically engineered bacteria produce human insulin for diabetes. Scientists hope in the future they will cure illnesses caused by a mistake in DNA, such as cystic fibrosis. Police can track down criminals if they leave something like hair or blood at a crime scene. Everyone's DNA is unique except identical twins, and the **genetic fingerprint** of this material can confirm if a suspect is guilty. Genetic fingerprinting can also show if two people are related. Archaeologists used it to prove that skeletons found in Russia were the remains of the Tsar and his family, killed during the 1919 revolution.

The Same But Different!

As well as showing our differences, DNA shows how much we are the same. Genes give us different coloured eyes, hair and skin, but 99.5% of your DNA is in the same order as everybody else's. 99% is the same as a chimpanzee's! The DNA of every living thing on Earth uses the same base chemicals. Because their bases are in a different order, the DNA of a worm or a tree makes different proteins from yours, and those proteins make different cells. All these cells developed from the first single-cell creatures formed three thousand million years ago, gradually evolving into new species to adapt to their environments. Only human beings have learned to analyse and use their DNA, and only we can learn to use that knowledge wisely.

The Magic Bullet

Have you ever had an earache or a sore throat? Sixty years ago people sometimes died from infections like these that doctors can now cure easily.

Under the Microscope

When Antoni van Leeuwenhoek (1632–1723) made a powerful microscope, he put his own spit under the lens. He saw tiny creatures he called **animalcules**. Some looked like rods (bacilli), some like balls (cocci) and some like spirals (spirilla). Today we call them **bacteria** and we know they can cause illness. Leeuwenhoek wrote about them in 1683, but nobody else could see them because he would not tell anybody how he made his lenses. Nobody knew how important this discovery was. They believed illness happened when fluids called **humours** in the body were out of balance.

By the nineteenth century, scientists had better microscopes. They could see bacteria but did not know where they came from. Many people believed they just appeared on their own.

The Discoveries of Louis Pasteur

In 1854, the French scientist Louis Pasteur (1822–1895) researched fermentation. He proved that bacteria getting into wine turned it sour and showed that heat killed them. To find out where the bacteria came from, Pasteur boiled soup in a glass flask and sealed it. The soup stayed fresh until he opened the flask, showing that bacteria must get into it from outside and did not grow on their own. He found that heating milk to a high temperature before bottling kept it fresh longer. We still call this process **pasteurisation**.

Pasteur found fewer bacteria in clean places like mountaintops, and more in dirty, crowded cities. He argued that diseases began when dangerous bacteria (germs) attacked the body from outside, just as unwanted bacteria turn wine or milk sour. Many scientists and doctors could not see how such tiny things could kill people.

Harmful Bacteria

Pasteur demonstrated his theory with the cattle disease anthrax. Robert Koch (1843–1910) had proved that a particular bacillus caused anthrax. Pasteur knew that a mild dose of a disease protected animals from further attacks, so he gave 25 sheep a weak dose. Later, he gave them and another 25 sheep a much stronger dose. He predicted that the second group would die. At the end of the experiment he showed his critics the bodies of the second group. The first group was still healthy. This work showed that bacteria cause infectious diseases.

Louis Pasteur

Doctors had to try to prevent diseases they could not cure. They knew that fewer women died from infections after childbirth if nurses washed their hands before moving from one patient to the next. However, at first they did not understand why. Surgeon Joseph Lister used a carbolic spray during operations to kill germs in the air and lost fewer patients to infected wounds. Later, Lister realised that hands and instruments also carried germs. He called the sprays that killed germs **antiseptics** from Latin words meaning "against decay". Hospitals became cleaner and safer places, but there were still few good medicines.

The Development of Antibiotics

Not all bacteria are harmful. We need some bacteria in our body to keep us healthy. Paul Ehrlich (1854–1915) aimed to find drugs that would work like a magic bullet, killing harmful germs without being dangerous to the patient. His work helped other scientists understand how our bodies fight disease, but nobody could produce Ehrlich's magic bullet.

Scientists stain bacteria to see them more clearly under a microscope. In 1932 Gerhard Domagk (1895–1964) found that red dye used to stain **Streptococcus** bacteria killed them. This led to the first medicines which could cure some infections, sulphonamides. This kind of medicine was called **antibiotic**, meaning "against life".

The Discovery of Penicillin

Four years earlier, in 1928, Alexander Fleming (1881–1955) cultured bacteria on several dishes. He left one aside by mistake. Later, he noticed a blue mould called **penicillium** growing on the dish. He was about to throw it away when he saw that the patches of mould had killed bacteria near them. Fleming found the mould killed bacteria causing meningitis and blood poisoning. He did not do experiments on animals or humans because extracts of the mould were hard to produce.

In 1938, Howard Florey (1898–1968), working in Oxford, followed up Fleming's lead. He and Ernst Chain (1906–1979) worked out which part of the mould killed bacteria and how to use it in medicines. They called this new medicine after the mould – **penicillin**.

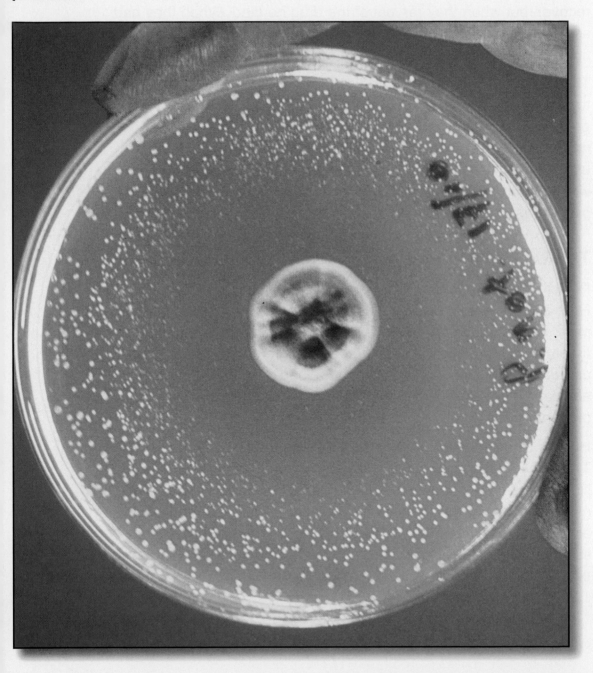

They treated their first patient in 1940 – a policeman dying of blood poisoning after scratching his finger on a rose thorn. Penicillium mould was difficult to grow and penicillin hard to extract. The researchers only had a tiny quantity, less than doctors use for one injection today, but they tried to save him. He began to recover, but when they ran out of the drug he died. When they had some more, they tried it on a boy dying from an eye infection. This time they had enough, and the boy recovered.

They grew the mould in bed bottles like those used in hospitals. It took a lot of mould to produce very little penicillin. Wartime problems in Britain made it hard to produce enough, so Florey moved the process to America. At first, only military people could use penicillin. After the war, once Dorothy Hodgkin and others worked out the structure of penicillin, drug companies could produce more active forms more cheaply.

The Use of Antibiotics

Penicillin works against many bacteria, but some resist it. Researchers look for other natural products and variations of penicillin to fight them. Drugs can now treat killer diseases like tuberculosis and leprosy. It only takes days to cure chest, throat and ear infections that used to mean a long stay in bed. However, antibiotic medicines do not work against viruses. Vaccination to prevent illness is still the best treatment for these.

Human beings have not always used these medicines wisely. They have sometimes taken antibiotics when they were not very ill. Farmers have used antibiotics on healthy animals to help them grow. Because of this, bacteria have evolved which resist common antibiotics, and doses now have to be much higher. Researchers still need to produce better drugs, but antibiotics are the nearest thing we have so far to a magic bullet.